WORDS *fitly* SPOKEN

Public Speaking for Women in Ministry

Formerly *Talk to Me, Lady*

BENETH PETERS JONES

BJU Press
Greenville, South Carolina
www.bjup.com

Library of Congress Cataloging-in-Publication Data

Jones, Beneth Peters, 1937-
    Words fitly spoken : public speaking for women in ministry : formerly,
    Talk to me, lady / Beneth Peters Jones.
        p.cm.
    ISBN 1-57924-597-8
    1. Preaching. 2. Women clergy. 3. Public speaking—Religious aspects—
Christianity. I. Jones, Beneth Peters, 1937-   . Talk to me, lady. II. Title.

BV4211.2 .J59 2001
251—dc21   2001025317

Note: The fact that materials produced by other publishers may be referred to
in this volume does not constitute an endorsement by Bob Jones University
Press of the content or theological position of materials produced by such publishers. The position of Bob Jones University Press, and of the University itself,
is well known. Any references and ancillary materials are listed as an aid to the
reader and in an attempt to maintain the accepted academic standards of the
publishing industry.

All Scripture is quoted from the Authorized King James Version.

Words Fitly Spoken

Cover and design by Jon Kopp
Composition by Carol Larson

©2001 Bob Jones University Press
Greenville, South Carolina 29614
First Edition ©1991 Bob Jones University Press

ISBN 1-57924-597-8

15 14 13 12 11 10 9 8 7 6 5 4 3 2 1

TABLE OF CONTENTS

❧

"Though I speak with the tongues of men and of angels, and have not charity, I am become as sounding brass, or a tinkling cymbal."

I CORINTHIANS 13:1

1

THE PURPOSE

THE PURPOSE

Is a booklet on public speaking really appropriate for Christian women? *Indeed!* Throughout the last several decades, women have become more and more vocal. Many aspects of that fact, however, are distressing.

- ❧ The *wrong* women are making themselves heard.
- ❧ They are saying the *wrong* things.
- ❧ They are having the *wrong* influence.

Their speech, thus, perniciously contributes to America's moral decay. It is, therefore, imperative that the *right* women become more active in saying the *right* things. For, as Proverbs 12:18 puts it, "the tongue of the wise is health."

But is a booklet on public speaking needed for women who may not consider themselves "speakers"—for example, preachers' wives? *Definitely!* Every Christian woman has a unique circle of influence. And each will have opportunities to speak within that circle. For the believer, that means opportunities to represent the Lord—to speak of Him and for Him. Opportunities that may occur among groups of other Christian women will include things such as

- ∾ A spur-of-the-moment testimony
- ∾ A Sunday school lesson
- ∾ A Bible study
- ∾ A mother/daughter banquet
- ∾ Retreat or seminar sessions

Other opportunities may be in a secular setting:

- ∾ A parent-teacher discussion
- ∾ A citizens group

Regardless of the speaking opportunity, we Christian women must consider and undertake such speech opportunities differently from unsaved women. We must be careful that

- ∾ We do not crusade for our "rights." We surrendered those to Jesus Christ when we accepted Him as Savior.
- ∾ We do not bewail or berate our lot as women. Instead, we recognize God's *goodness* in allowing us to be who we are.
- ∾ We do not adopt a masculine manner or voice. Instead, we conduct ourselves as ladies: we maintain and exemplify femininity. And we speak to our audience woman to woman, heart to heart.
- ∾ We do not seek to exalt ourselves, exhibit our scholarship, tout our professional accomplish-

ments, parade our training, or set ourselves up as examples of successful living.

Rather, our intention is twofold: to **help** our listeners and, always, to **exalt** the Lord Jesus Christ.

Can this little book on public speaking then actually help an ordinary, run-of-the-mill Christian woman—someone who has never taken even one speech class? *Yes!* In the first place, *each one of us is an ordinary, run-of-the-mill Christian woman.* Some of us have just been pushed or pulled onto the speech platform a bit more often or earlier than some others. In the second place, every one of us "speaks" on a daily basis. Find us among friends after church or in the grocery store, and we can speak convincingly, freely, dynamically, and dramatically whether it is to one person or to a group. So to put this natural gift into a more formal setting requires only a few relatively simple principles.

That is the **purpose** behind this book: the reason I am writing it; the reason, I pray, it can be used of God to help you toward "a word fitly spoken" (Proverbs 25:11).

*"The tongue of the wise useth knowledge aright:
but the mouth of fools poureth out foolishness."*

PROVERBS 15:2

2

THE FEAR

THE~ FEAR

The very thought of standing in front of people to speak strikes terror to your heart, right? You have plenty of company. Surveys show that the fear of public speaking is second only to the fear of dying! Obviously, then, this terror does not mark you as unusual; it simply confirms your humanity.

The manifestations of stage fright are many. Different people suffer different symptoms but all are relatively universal. You may be affected in one or more of the following ways.

- Racing heart
- Shortness of breath
- Dry mouth
- Cold, clammy hands
- Tremors of hands and knees
- Nausea

Although these discomforts are not pleasant for anyone, *neither are they fatal.* Survivors everywhere confirm the happy truth for the world; otherwise, our ranks would have been bereft long ago of the finest musicians, dramatic

9

artists, and public figures. Although it is hard to believe, even seasoned, apparently effortless, platform people battle fear.

For the Christian, stage fright must be seen first of all from a scriptural perspective. The Bible tells us, literally hundreds of times, to live courageously. One verse I have found to be particularly applicable to the challenge of speaking is Psalm 27:14: "Wait on the Lord: be of good courage, and he shall strengthen thine heart." Notice that this verse tells us to *exercise courage* before we *receive strength*. We prefer to make it work in reverse order; we want God to give us the strength and then we'll find the courage. God also promises "grace to help in time of need" (Hebrews 4:16). The grace does not come until the moment of need.

Often a large part of any speaker's fear is forgetting or getting lost from the intended material. An anonymous writer put it this way: "The human brain starts working the moment you are born and never stops until you stand up to speak in public." A wonderful scriptural antidote for the forgetfulness is Proverbs 16:3: "Commit thy works unto the Lord, *and thy thoughts shall be established.*"

A speaker's fear can also be the result of a wrong focus. Our fearfulness comes when we are focusing on ourselves and the potential for self-humiliation and not upon God and the truth that He has called us to this difficult task.

We must remember that "faithful is he that calleth you, who also will do it" (I Thessalonians 5:24).

Added to the scriptural perspective is a practical key for combating nervousness: use it. Those troublesome indications of fear can actually signal a kindling, not a killing. Adrenaline is being pumped into your body. This "nervous energy" can be translated into enthusiasm and the desire to communicate. It sparks effective communication by

- Ordering the heart to circulate blood more quickly.
- Supplying the whole body with extra energy.
- Stimulating the brain.
- Enhancing the entire being with an intensity that focuses audience attention.

Obviously, then, the secret is to *use* all those adrenaline-produced extras rather than be *unstrung* by them. It's a matter of control and direction.

In my years of teaching and speaking I have met only one woman who felt no stage fright. Interestingly, she was herself a fright on the stage, lackluster and ineffective. She had no internal energy on which to draw and no fervor with which to hold her audience's attention.

Finally, attitude can play a strategic part in the intensity of stage fright. If your mindset is one of dread—"I *have* to do this"—you increase the level of fear. If, instead, we change to an attitude of "I *get* to do this," we loosen terror's grip.

Therefore, do plenty of talking to yourself before you talk to others; deny the negative attitude and choose the positive one. The difference will not evaporate stage fright, but it prevents it from becoming paralyzing fear.

If we are filled with a spirit of fear, we can be assured it is not from God. He has promised us power and a sound mind. That means a mind that is not controlled by those nervous feelings we call stage fright.

"For God has not given us the spirit of fear, but of power, and of love, and of a sound mind."

II TIMOTHY 1:7

3

THE PATTERN

THE PATTERN

A study of female speakers can be very informative and helpful. If you have never made a personal study, I recommend you start one. Each time a woman gets up to talk, watch; listen; and make mental notes.

- ∾ Did she catch and hold your attention? If so, how?
- ∾ Did she present her material clearly? Could you easily follow her main points?
- ∾ Did what you saw and sensed about her as a person back up her words?
- ∾ Was she effective as a communicator? Did she convey a pleasant, honest, woman-to-woman spirit? Why or why not?

Although listeners can defy or deflect a speaker's presentation, the one who is speaking has the primary responsibility for effective communication. The speaker must make the listener want to listen. Begin making fair, analytical evaluations of women speakers in your personal world. *Do not* get negatively critical; always sympathize with those who are less than effective, appreciating the fact that they tried. You should watch, listen, and make your observations of others count positively toward your own preparation and presentation.

As you analyze, *consider but do not copy.* The things that can be copied from anyone are surface aspects—mannerisms, stance, facial expressions, and so forth. Though they fit the original person using them, they will be misfits on anyone else. While recognizing and adopting effective techniques of speech, *always be yourself as a speaker.* It is the wonderful "plus" of your own *absolutely unique person* that will help make you effective as you talk.

Just as you can profit from studying positive models, you can also profit from studying negative ones. What are the characteristics of the speaker that make your mind wander, that cause you to wish you were somewhere else? If you are aware of them, you can avoid them when you speak. Here are a few characteristics and practices that can kill meaningful communication:

- Lack of enthusiasm
- Lack of freshness
- Vocal monotony
- Performance rather than communication
- Needless repetition

Today's Christian woman—whatever her walk of life—is far too busy and much too burdened to sacrifice her valuable time to a boring speaker. Time being bored is time being wasted. We who speak carry a double responsibility in time stewardship: our own and our listeners'.

"To the law and to the testimony: if they speak not according to this word, it is because there is no light in them."

ISAIAH 8:20

4

THE FOCUS

THE FOCUS

When you are preparing a topic for any occasion, it is wise to remember that women are emotionally oriented; that lends distinctive character to feminine audiences. The woman speaker must use emotional appeals with responsibility and restraint.

LAUGHTER

First, a word about the joyful emotions. Some Christians get the distorted idea that to smile is sinful, to laugh unspiritual. What a shame! We who know the blessed freedom from sin's penalty through the shed blood of Jesus Christ are told to live *joyfully.* How can that oft-repeated precept be interpreted as *mournfully*? Fortunately, those who choose not to laugh are in the minority among the Christian population. For most of us, an opportunity to smile and laugh is welcome.

There have been a number of studies showing that a happy outlook on life and an active sense of humor are beneficial to health. Long before such studies, the writer of Proverbs said, "A merry heart doeth good like a medicine" (Proverbs 17:22). Laughter might also be thought of as oil on the hinges of the heart's door. That is why it is an excellent tool for a speaker. Even in handling the most serious, deep, or delicate subjects, carefully employed humor can be strategic. It can bring both enjoyment and relaxation; it warms the heart and encourages interpersonal bonding. As one anonymous wag put it, "A good thing to have up your sleeve is a funny bone."

When speaking, use humor wisely and sparingly. It is always wise to avoid anything sacrilegious or offensive. It is also wise to poke fun at yourself rather than at others. Use humor sparingly so that laughter is a delicate, wonderful spice that will enhance the impact of thoughtful, soul-probing segments.

Humor works both ways by relaxing both the speaker and the audience. In particular, it can smooth the awkward opening moments of a talk. That's the reason so many effective preachers tell a joke as they begin a sermon.

There are other types of humor in addition to jokes, however. These include puns and word play, satire and irony, understatement and exaggeration. It is always best to know what type of humor you handle best. For instance, I cannot tell a joke. If I try, nobody laughs; the hearers give me only stony stares or sympathetic side glances. But the Lord has given me the ability to find humor in common, everyday occurrences; by simply sharing those I can make people laugh. Your comic strength may lie, instead, in hilarious word play. The point is don't try to be like anyone else; instead, invite laughter into your talks in the unique way your own personality dictates.

When incorporating humor into your speech, remember that unless you intend *only* to entertain and, therefore, to use slapstick, do not break over into silliness. In trying to use humor, some speakers leap off the high dive of restraint into the pool of the ridiculous. No one emerges with anything worthwhile.

Also do not get swept away by your own funniness; it makes the funny *un*funny. When you use humor, it is a little like handing the audience a box filled with laughter: after opening it, you need to stand back and let *them* have the enjoyment.

TEARS

Just as we women are quick to sweep into gales of laughter, so too are we easily moved to tears. After all, what red-blooded female does not enjoy a good cry?

The sympathetic appeal is legitimate in speaking, but it, too, must be *guardedly used*. This is particularly important when speaking to women because of their emotional susceptibility. It is best not to use emotion as the primary appeal in talking: that is manipulative—and manipulated emotion is empty. Our purpose *to help* women is not served by simply making them cry.

Think about how unsaved women speakers manipulate emotion. They work to stir anger by using inflammatory words, and they strive to heighten frustration by pointing to our supposedly denied "rights." Whipped into emotional frenzy, the deluded troops march forward, trampling underfoot both common sense and rational thought.

We, of course, recognize and dislike such tactics. But even some Christian speakers follow a similar course. Any speaker likes to sense the audience responding, and *tears are an observable response.* The Christian woman speaker, however, must not feed her own feeling of success by making her audience cry.

There might be a time now and then when, in sharing a personal experience, you as the speaker get choked up with emotion. As far as is possible, prevent the danger by allowing a healing time span between an experience and your sharing it with an audience. For example, I mentioned the death of our first baby to a group of student wives less than two years after our loss. It was too soon; I lost emotional control. The lesson was painful for speaker and audience alike.

When emotionalism "sneaks up" on you unawares, pause and regain control. To the best of your ability, do not cry on the platform. Uncontrolled emotion embarrasses an

audience. It also misuses them in that tears inspire tears—
purposeless tears—in women hearers.

MOTIVATION

The purpose in persuasive or inspirational speaking is *to motivate:* to motivate change of mind or change of life. Human change must be preceded by decision making. There are three things a speaker can use to influence decisions: Emotion, reason or logic, and the Word of God.

Obviously, as we have just discussed, the *worst and weakest* of these is emotion. Emotional "decisions" are often simply *reactions*; as such, they seldom produce durable results. An element of emotion certainly is valid in spiritual matters. The Bible speaks much of the heart of man. But emotion should be the smallest part of a speaker's appeal. The major emphasis must be Scripture— that perfect, eternal, all-powerful Truth. The second-largest part of the appeal should be to reason. Christian women need to think soberly and deeply about the problem areas in their lives. Unfortunately, women attending conferences and seminars too often are given simplistic formulas and answers based on an emotional response, *none of which work.*

So, when you speak to your audience, let them know that you have done plenty of good, hard thinking yourself, and make them think along with you. Let them see into your heart and your humanity, but do not blubber about it. Do not give them eye-popping or tear-jerking details: the former is sensationalism, and the latter is sentimentality. And please, *always,* point them ultimately to the Word of God and the God of the Word.

"And he hath put a new song in my mouth,
even praise unto our God: many shall see it,
and fear, and shall trust in the Lord."

PSALM 40:3

5

THE
SUBSTANCE

THE SUBSTANCE

Just as there are different kinds of opportunities for speaking, there are, of course, different kinds of talks. They fall into four main categories:

- ∿ To inform
- ∿ To convince
- ∿ To inspire
- ∿ To entertain

Almost any topic may be treated any of these four ways, depending upon how you select and arrange the material.

As an example, let us consider the broad topic of "Birds." In an *informative* talk you would relate interesting facts about birds, simply seeking to extend your listeners' knowledge. Such a speech would be appropriate for a bird watcher's club. For a *persuasive* talk you might focus upon the dangers songbirds face in daily existence, urging your hearers to take personal interest in preserving the local songbird population. An opportunity to present such a speech might occur in a local community meeting. At a ladies meeting you may choose an *inspirational* talk drawing analogies between a bird's worry-free, song-filled life and the prescribed Christian walk. And at an informal party you may wish to *entertain* by sharing observations of humorous bird behavior, plus thematic comic poetry and song texts.

After you have determined which type of speech is appropriate for the occasion, you need to narrow your topic, research it, and formulate an outline. For example, you might narrow the topic "birds" down to bluebirds. Sample outlines for each of the different types of talks, might look like these:

Informative: Bluebirds

    I. Their physical structure
   II. Their habitats
 III. Their lifestyle
 IV. Their value

Persuasive: Bluebirds Endangered!

    I. Local depopulation
   II. Evidences of their demise
 III. Environmental/aesthetic impact
 IV. Personal responsibility

Inspirational: A Bluebird's Heart

    I. A fragile heart
   II. A singing heart
 III. A trusting heart

Entertaining: A Bluebird Gone Purple

  I. Oh, those boredom blues

 II. Painting everything purple

III. Paying the consequences

In most instances, however, our purpose as Christian women speaking to Christian women will be to inspire. High-sounding though that may be, it basically means *to encourage.* Inspirational speaking offers many ways to reveal and exalt the Lord, numberless "gates" through which we can move toward that goal. These gates are our *topics* or *subjects*.

Perhaps the most common speaking opportunity for the Christian woman is a testimony. Every born-again Christian should be "ready always to give an answer" (I Peter 3:15) with regard to her own personal testimony. A testimony embodies its own topic: Christ's working in our lives to save and sanctify. The effectiveness of that presentation can be helped by three simple but important considerations:

- Let the telling spring from your heart; it is best not to memorize what you want to say.

- Keep the telling of God's grace sincere, clear, and brief. Be careful not to sound like a wind-up talk toy or to ramble.

- For those with whom you fellowship often, tell of one *specific* recent working of God in your life.

∾ Be sure to put the spotlight on *the Lord,* not
overdo the "I" and thereby produce a brag-I-mony.

Practically speaking, an old adage puts it bluntly but well:
Stand up, speak up, shut up.

Should your speaking opportunities expand beyond personal testimonies, you may be asked to speak for a special
occasion that has a theme or celebrates a season. When
that is the case, you will have the theme to help direct
your topic choice. Your only decision then will be the
specific approach you want to take. But no matter what
direction the occasion points, it is important to be thor-
ough and diligent in selecting and preparing a topic. Here
are the basic steps to follow.

SELECT

Whenever you are faced with an open subject choice,
begin with prayer. Ask the Lord to show you the topic
gate through which you can best glorify Him for this particular occasion. His direction will not come in lightning
script across the sky, but through quiet impressions upon
your heart. Often the best topics are found in lessons
taught to us by God in our daily lives.

While seeking God's guidance, put feet to your search.
Look for something that has been impressed upon you,
not for something to impress an audience. A topic that
has meaning to *you personally*

∾ Enriches your preparation.

∾ Enlists your energy.

∾ Insures your involvement while speaking.

∾ Entices audience attention.

Consider the small things. In order to be good, subjects do not have to be exotic, dangerous, or exciting. The motivation in inspirational talks should be to help the hearers and exalt the Lord. Women are best helped by having someone come alongside them *in the simple, small struggles of life;* God is likewise exalted as we share the reality of *His sufficiency in those struggles.*

Put real effort into your topic search. Rather than take the first idea that comes along (or an outline from another speaker), let your mind range far and wide among the lessons and experiences you have had in life. Has there been one area in particular where God recently underlined His teaching for you? That is often the way He directs toward topic choice.

RESEARCH

Having chosen your topic "gate," learn everything you can about it. Although personal interest and involvement are vital, do not limit yourself to those. Extend your knowledge by doing as many of the following as possible.

Look up word meanings

Do not reserve your dictionary just for unfamiliar word meanings. Definitions of commonly used words can sometimes open exciting possibilities and add dimensions of interest to your talk.

Read and take notes

Commentaries are helpful in clarifying Scripture passages. Bible dictionaries and encyclopedias can reveal little-known facts that will add new dimensions to your presentation. Magazines and books on current topics are valuable sources of statistics and up-to-date information.

Listen

As you listen to the testimonies and trials of others, you may find illustrations for the truths that you plan to present. Someone else's perspective on a familiar topic can open new understanding.

Observe

Not only the people around us, but all of God's creation can reveal truths that show us who God is and how He works in our lives.

Collect poems, statistics, and illustrations

When looking for illustrations, be fussy; don't settle for the first thing you find in a book of speaker illustrations. An effective illustration meets certain qualifications.

- ∾ It should *accurately* and succinctly put the desired point into memorable form.
- ∾ It should be up-to-date. Many illustration books are ancient, presenting stories that are simplistic, sentimental, and out of touch with modern life.
- ∾ It should be fresh. Some illustrations earned retirement long ago; they have become hackneyed through overuse.
- ∾ The best illustrations come from your own life experience and observation; they will be fresh and branded with your unique personal perspective.

Conduct an informal survey

Ask the opinions of others on topic-related issues. You will find a wide variety of views that you may incorporate into your speech.

REDUCE

Research uncovers material that supports and develops your original idea. In fact, generally you will find that there is *too much* to cover within your time limit. Good! Now narrow your focus. Remember, your intention is not to mow a ten-acre plot, but to blaze a single track from your topic gate to your goal. It is important to remember that a topic that needs reduction is better than one requiring padding. Women listeners are quick to recognize verbal padding. In fact, if research fails to uncover abundant supportive materials, *you would be wise to change topics.*

PLAN

So there you are—the Lord has led and you have worked to build the right topic gate. Now, how do you choose an effective path to the goal of exalting the Lord and helping your hearers?

First of all, identify your goal very clearly by making a written statement of your purpose. It might look something like this: "I want to reveal the Lord and help my hearers by showing how God can work through our handicaps." That becomes the goal upon which your eyes will be fixed throughout the hours of preparation.

Next, begin tracing a possible pathway: get your ideas down on paper in rough outline form. Don't concern yourself with correct outline form at this point; simply organize your research into groups of like information. You may even wish to cut your notes into strips between pieces of information. This way you can physically rearrange your information without having to recopy every time you wish to change the order.

Once you have determined a basic order for your information, there is a basic formula for determining the main points of your outline. Remember your speech is the pathway that leads from the topic gate to your goal. Therefore, each main point in your outline should mark one major landmark along the way. The subpoints in your outline will provide the scenic details that make each of those spots noteworthy. Remember, however, if you use everything you have collected, your speech pathway will wind and wander. You don't want to weary your audience with much speaking. Instead, you want to take *the most direct, yet scenic, route from your topic gate to your goal.*

As you work along this pathway, the first obstacle you encounter may be the boggy ground of excessive materials. For instance, you may have five poems in your talk folder; all five say something good about the subject. You need one firm plank to take you over the bog: the single *best* poem of the lot. A good rule of thumb is this: An outline with more than five or six main points usually signals excess. Eliminate and refine!

As you develop your pathway, there may be underbrush of outdated or confusing statistics. Do not get lost in the thicket! Be sure any figures you use are up-to-date and support your point accurately. Statistics can be twisted to say anything, and often they are used for that purpose by less-than-honest speakers.

Even though you have narrowed your topic and established your main points, you may still find yourself meandering from side to side, using a great many subpoints and sub-subpoints. You are still trying to cover too much territory. You must continue to narrow down your information.

Analyze your materials carefully. Which of the collected facts, experience(s), and illustration(s) lead *most surely and steadily* toward the goal? Put everything else aside and stick to those. Throughout your initial preparation—

- ∾ Give everything the test.
- ∾ Choose the best.
- ∾ Discard the rest.

Remember as you plan that the beginning moments of any speech are critical for both you and the audience. It is very important, therefore, to *plan* your opening. This requires a two-part consideration.

First, you should respond to the welcoming introduction given you and express gratitude for being invited. Obviously, you cannot know ahead of time how you will be introduced. So—for the beginning of the opening, listen to her introduction, take a key from the occasion, and blend the two into a *very short* preliminary, mentioning

- ∾ The introduction
- ∾ The invitation to speak
- ∾ The occasion or group

Then move on into the planned introduction for your talk. **This can be memorized.** You are opening your topic gate and you want to give it a good, firm shove. In order to do that, your introduction needs to

- ◦ Capture attention (bring the listeners to join you at the gate).
- ◦ Present a preview (give them a glimpse of the path ahead).

It is essential that you get the attention of the audience right away. You may wish to include one of these good attention-getters in your introduction.

- ◦ Pose a question to the audience.
- ◦ Read a short, pertinent poem.
- ◦ Tell a brief, illustrative story.
- ◦ Use a visual aid.

The combination of a clear opening response plus your rehearsed introduction will begin to thaw stage fright's icy hold as you control your heart palpitations, steady your voice, and get your mind into forward gear.

CONCLUSION

From the moment of introduction you are off, taking your listener with you, toward the goal. You will travel the pathway together. All along the way you will draw the listeners attention to each landmark and scenic view.

But after you have traveled the topic path together for the allotted time, do not disappear. You need to provide a conclusion to your talk. The idea is this: As you stand at the goal, you must ask your audience to do one of several things:

- ∾ Look back along the path and consider. Reiterate the main points. By repeating your primary thoughts, you help your audience review and remember.

- ∾ Contemplate the goal itself. Summarize what has been said. Restating your purpose reinforces the goal for your listener.

- ∾ Stand at the goal and face forward encouraged, rebuked, or challenged by the path you've shared. Leave the audience with a question or entreat your hearers to make a decision.

- ∾ Provide a final quiet thought. Encapsulate with a brief story or poem.

As in the introduction, keep the conclusion brief. Preparing and rehearsing your conclusion as well as your introduction will keep you from struggling for a final sentence. But once you have said your final word, **then quit talking.** *It is not necessary to say "thank you."*

"Set a watch, O Lord, before my mouth;
keep the door of my lips."

PSALM 141:3

6

THE PRACTICE

THE PRACTICE

Anything but a spur-of-the-moment testimony or discussion participation will be the type of talk called "extemporaneous." That just means *prepared but not memorized.*

You need to follow your roughly mapped pathway a number of times yourself before showing it to others. Without trying to set any specific wording, practice *aloud* at least *three times.* That is a must for several reasons:

- A talk is not a talk when it is just on paper.
- Oral practice reveals rough spots that need to be reworked.
- Practicing alone spares your audience from practicing on them.
- Assuming the posture, voice, and so forth of the actual talk helps get body and brain prepared for the real thing.

Practice is preparation, and preparation reduces stage fright.

As you practice orally, you may decide that some platform memory prompts would be helpful. A successful journey from gate to goal may require a few signposts.

A skeleton outline is always a helpful prompt. Each point and subpoint should be no more than a *very* few words. These few words should act as a trigger for the main idea you wish to remember.

The physical form of your outline is up to you. Some speakers prefer regular 8½"×11" notebook paper; others choose 3"×5" or 4"×6" index cards. I personally prefer notebook paper that measures 5½"×8½". Make your own choice according to what is best for you. Be sure the information is visible and easy to read. (*Brief, occasional* glances are all you get!) Also be sure that the format you choose is easy for you to handle. Although some speakers manage note cards well, cards rebel against me: they get wildly out of order or fall onto the floor.

One very helpful tip for quickly locating outline points while speaking is *color-coding*. Main points highlighted in one color, subpoints in a second, and sub-subpoints in a third are easily distinguishable by both your eyes and brain.

When you are preparing and practicing your presentation, it is also wise to remember and consider that time is a key factor. If you exceed your time limit, your effectiveness can be hindered, and you will lose the attention of your audience.

Think of time limits as just that: limits. The organizers of that event are not making suggestions; *they are telling you when to stop!* One of the most important responsibilities any speaker has is to honor time limits.

Whenever you accept a speaking opportunity, find out right away what the time limits are. Time boundaries will serve as a guideline as you look for topic ideas and do research. They also will help you in the rehearsal process. As you practice aloud with one eye on the clock, you will find that often you must delete some things and condense others.

When you reach the speaker's stand, always look at the clock or your wristwatch and make two mental notes: your starting time and your stopping time.

"But," you say, "what if . . ."

- You get so engrossed in your presentation that you cannot cover all the material? You, not the audience, must suffer the consequences more! Even if you have wandered so badly from your outline that you must skip points, do so—*and quit on time.*

- The invitation was given with only a vague indication of time limit: "about 35 or 40 minutes"? *Aim for the shorter, and never go beyond the longer.*

Time is of the essence in any speaking situation. Occasionally, last minute changes may require some major on-the-spot adjustments for you. For instance, in retreat, seminar, or banquet programs, the preliminaries may cut into your speaking time. So *condense*! No matter how badly others may derail the schedule, do your dead-level best to get it back on track, *unless told specifically* to adjust your closing time. Even when that is done, keep your talk on the *short* side.

Never consider encroachment upon your time as an insult; think of it as a challenge. Rise to that challenge, and put your material into an effective shorthand form.

And whoever you are, whatever your name, position, or title, do not think that importance circumvents time limits. That attitude expresses enormous egotism; yet, unfortunately, it is common in Christian circles.

Brevity will pay dividends not only in audience appreciation but also in their ability to focus upon and follow you down your pathway of thoughts. As an audience member, you doubtless agree with the old saying "Brevity is the soul of wit." As the speaker, you must believe it just as strongly—and *demonstrate* it!

Research, development, and practice are interesting and challenging in themselves; but the time comes for leaving the preliminaries and getting on to the real task, your moments on the platform: the actual speech itself and **you**, the speaker.

> *"The preparations of the heart in man, and*
> *the answer of the tongue is from the Lord."*

PROVERBS 16:1

7

THE IMPRESSION

THE IMPRESSION

How do you form your first impression of anyone? By what you see, don't you? Your listeners will "size you up" the same way. That being the case, your appearance deserves careful attention before platform time. Remember, you are representing not only yourself but also the Lord before that group of ladies. The first impression they have of you will often determine how well they will listen and heed what you say. I believe that a female audience presents a special challenge to a speaker in the matter of appearance. Let's face it: we women generally tend to be less accepting and more critical—particularly to other women. Too, we see details more readily than do most men.

GOOD GROOMING

Basic good grooming is a must. That does not mean wearing expensive clothes; it simply means *clean* and *neat*. Good grooming is essential for each one of us who claims to represent Jesus Christ, the one who is altogether lovely! Whether we are on the platform or in the grocery store, our appearance speaks volumes about how we view ourselves and the one we serve.

PLATFORM DRESS

For anything but spur-of-the-moment talks, think carefully about what you should wear. The Christian woman should follow these important guidelines for platform dress.

Modesty

With regard to modesty, probably the greatest failure comes in the matter of skirt length. A skirt that is modest when you are standing may not be modest when you are sitting on a raised platform. Also be aware of the cling of fabric, the tightness, or the transparency.

Attractiveness

Clothing worn by the speaker should be attractive in two ways: personally becoming to her (contributing to her positive outlook) and visually pleasing to the audience (contributing to their positive attention).

In order to predispose the audience in your favor, be sure that your outfit is attractive *in the right way.* In color it is best to opt for subdued tones. Red, for instance, is hard to look at for any extended length of time; what's more, researchers tell us it tends to arouse negative reactions. Consider pattern as well; certain stripes and dots can be dizzying, and bold patterns call undue attention to themselves.

As for style, while choosing that which is becoming to your person, be careful to avoid extremes of any kind. Specifically

- ∾ Very strict tailoring conveys a stern image.
- ∾ Ruffles, if overdone, say "mental lightweight."
- ∾ A style *either* obviously outdated *or* too up-to-the-minute invites feminine resistance.

In both color and style, choose that which directs attention to your face.

Appropriateness

Appropriate clothing enables you to "fit in" with regard to formality, activities, weather, and overall social atmosphere. For example, a snowstorm in July would catch anyone unawares; however, wearing sleeveless cottons to a January camp retreat in Maine reveals a mental elevator that stops before it reaches the top floor!

Because different areas of the country and even different church groups vary in what they consider appropriate dress, it is always a good idea to ask about specifics before packing your wardrobe.

Realizing that a female audience will scrutinize you may intimidate you. Let that foreknowledge work for you by serving as an incentive to *look yourself over thoroughly* long before they see you. Stand and sit in front of a full-length mirror in the outfit(s) you are considering. If anything about the outfit is doubtful, don't wear it. You should be safe in your choice if the following descriptive words are added to the basic requirement of modesty:

- ∾ Sensible
- ∾ Subdued
- ∾ Simple

Your mirror has a very important message for you before you try to get one across to someone else; it is wise to heed it!

"Prove all things; hold fast that which is good."

I THESSALONIANS 5:21

8

THE APPEARANCE

THE APPEARANCE

Good grooming and proper clothing, no matter how thoughtfully chosen, are only part of a speaker's appearance. How a woman carries herself also sends a visual message, which can positively reinforce the spoken word. The way you sit, stand, and walk influences how you—and your message—are received.

Good carriage begins with good posture. Simply put, you will carry yourself well if you adhere to the following:

- **Head** rides with ears directly over your shoulders, with chin parallel to the floor.
- **Shoulders** are erect but not stiff, relaxed but not slumped.
- **Chest** is held high, not drooping into the waistline.
- **Spine** is upright, with no pronounced *S* curve.
- **Pelvis** is tucked under, eliminating "back porch" and swayback.
- **Knees** are slightly flexed, not stiff or locked.
- **Feet** point straight ahead, with no more than nine to ten inches between them. (When actually speaking, you will look more dynamic if one foot is a bit

forward and most of your weight is on that forward foot.)

Tip-to-toe alignment should not begin and end at the mi-
crophone, however; it should be an *always* thing.

Walking is simply putting good posture into motion. For
a speaker, the challenge of getting from her seat to the
platform gracefully can be complicated by two particular
environmental hazards: steps and chairs. However, you
can come out the winner against those challenges.

If you sit in the audience prior to speaking and must walk
up onto the platform, even a two-step rise can look like
Mount Everest, but even Mount Everest has been con-
quered. Use the following as guidelines for a graceful as-
cent:

- Avoid presenting a full back view to the audience.
  Instead, engineer a three-quarter route; the
  straight-on back presentation is not the best for
  anyone!

- Do not drop your chin to watch the steps as you
  mount them. *Do* look at the stairs carefully from
  your seat in the audience; check their width,
  height, and number. When it is actually time to
  climb them, put that analysis to work by having
  your *brain* remind your muscles and joints what to
  do while your *eyes* look straight ahead onto the
  platform.

꙯ Adjust your feet as necessary, according to the steps' width. Platform steps often seem to have been constructed only for those with size three feet! It is better to place size sevens *at an angle* than to count disaster by teetering up and down on tiptoe.

Greater than the stairs scare is the challenge of the chair. Platform chairs (my generic term for all types of platform seating) are notorious opponents. I have met *very* few that were even slightly friendly. Someday I would like to find the supposedly "average" person for whom such seats have been designed. The anatomy of that fellow must be a scientific wonder!

Platform seats may be classified as follows:

꙯ Rock hard
꙯ Slushy soft
꙯ New-wax slick
꙯ Splintery
꙯ Too high
꙯ Too low

It is no wonder, then, that the woman speaker, concerned with graceful carriage and modest appearance, takes small delight in dealing with THE CHAIR. Basically, my advice must boil down to "Do the best you can, dear." But these principles for "normal" sitting may shore you up for the battle.

- ∾ Maintain good posture while going into and getting out of sitting's "fold."

- ∾ Do not keep your eyes fixed on the chair as you take your seat; to do that you will have to twist like a pretzel.

- ∾ As you approach the seat, gauge essential elements of its position, height, depth, and material.

- ∾ With body and head erect, turn as soon as you reach the chair; feel the front of its seat with your backmost leg.

- ∾ Lower yourself into the seat with back straight, head erect, and *thigh muscles* doing all the work.

- ∾ Do not collapse in the middle.

- ∾ Do not labor with your shoulder.

- ∾ Take the most propitious position on the chair seat for your soon-coming rise. (Not back too deep, but not "perched" precariously.)

- ∾ Sit three-quarters to the audience, not straight on.

- ∾ Keep knees and ankles TOGETHER. While that rule applies at all times, it is *especially* important on the platform!

- ∾ Never cross your knees. If you must cross something to cut down on the shakes of stage fright, cross ankles only.

If you imagine the above demonstrated on a video, simply reversing the film will show you how to rise from a chair.

Once you are on the platform and on your feet, the next approach is to the podium. This seems simple enough, but a simple tip might help you. When approaching the speaker's stand from the side, lead with the foot farthest from the audience. That keeps the body in an "open" position and says, in effect, "I'm looking forward to talking with you."

Once you are safely and gracefully established at the podium, then what? Open the topic gate and lead the way. Be sure, however, to involve yourself physically in what you are saying, right from the first word. Don't be immobilized as a speaker.

If you're not sure what kind of physical involvement might be appropriate, watch yourself and your acquaintances in casual conversation. Do words and sentences issue from deadpan faces or unmoving bodies? No. We normally involve our whole selves in what we are saying. Our faces change expression according to our speech content. Our bodies tense or relax. Our hands wave, point, open, ball into fists, or slice the air.

That same kind of physical involvement should be part of public speaking, but stage fright tends to mummify both face and body. Making yourself move helps loose the bands of fright. If you are a newcomer to an area, how readily would you accept complicated directions from someone who only *told* you how to go? Not very. But if that person *physically leads* down the path you would be more apt to follow.

Not only does bodily involvement help you get your message across in the general sense, but gestures also clarify and punctuate what you are saying. They emphasize, describe, and complete. So make your hands work for you; do not let them hide in your pockets or behind your back, clutch the podium, or flutter and flap meaninglessly.

These physical considerations may seem insignificant, but they are not. If you *appear* positive, controlled, and enthusiastic, your bearing will help convince your audience as well as you. Research tells us that *the greatest part of any person-to-person communication is nonverbal*. Therefore, the Christian woman speaker wants to make the following nonverbal statements:

- ∾ "I'm eager to share with you."
- ∾ "I'm interested in you and glad to be with you."
- ∾ "This subject is important."
- ∾ "I feel the Lord has impressed this message on my heart."

While you use your voice to speak to the audience, use your hands, face, and body tonicity to be sure your words are fitly spoken.

"For man looketh on the outward appearance."

I SAMUEL 16:7

9

THE CONTACT

THE CONTACT

There you are . . . standing in front of an audience, with many pairs of eyes fixed upon you. Having checked the clock, where should you look next? *Into the eyes that are looking at you.* And keep looking there throughout your talk.

Have you ever sat in an audience listening to a speaker who avoided eye contact? Maddening, wasn't it? Genuine communication is an eye-to-eye matter. If, for instance, we want a small child to *really* get what we are going to say, we command, "Now look me in the eye." Whenever you talk to a group, imagine each woman is saying the same thing to you. In essence, she is. She wants to feel you are talking *to* her, not *at* her.

Eye contact says several important things to a listener:

- ❧ You are honest and can be trusted.
- ❧ You have a personal interest in me, the listener.
- ❧ You recognize the two-way nature of communication.

Looking your audience in the eye does not mean that you gaze intently at one or two on the front row and let it go at that. You need to include everyone at some time during the course of your talk. It works like this:

- ∾ Establish eye contact with the first person upon whom your glance falls. Keep looking at her just long enough to make the "Yes,-I'm-talking-to-you" and "Okay-I'm-listening" connection.
- ∾ Move on to another individual and do the same thing.
- ∾ Follow that person-to-person pattern throughout your talk.
- ∾ In areas far from the platform, let two or three eye connections serve for a section.
- ∾ Areas awkwardly located on either side of the main floor or a balcony should be included occasionally.
- ∾ Eye contact is not only important in that it helps you get across what you want to say, but it is also important *to you* throughout your talk.

As you sense you are talking to individuals, your fear of "the crowd" diminishes.

Expressions and reactions feed you constant, valuable information. Some listeners may show hostility; others challenge; yet, a few (bless them!) will "key in" to what you're saying and eagerly await more. Discouragement will be telegraphed by some; spiritual hunger by others.

And so it goes—silent, strong messages coming to you along that strategic communication cable: eye contact. Do not fail to plug into that cable!

While a great deal is said through eye contact and bodily action, we think of speaking as being primarily a thing of *voice*.

And so it is. Our voices, and the ability to speak, are wonderful gifts from our loving Creator God. Like so many other things, though, we take our voices for granted unless something impairs them or we have to speak to an audience.

BREATH SUPPORT

Voice is produced as air rising from the lungs passes over vibrating vocal folds in the throat. In normal activities all of that seems natural and effortless. But in a public speaking situation the combination of stage fright and the need to project can put strain on the vocal mechanism. The extra effort to reach the volume needed at such times may come from the worst possible place: the throat. Instead, the added push should originate in your midsection, where the airflow is controlled. This is the technique known as diaphragmatic breathing. If you are unfamiliar with this type of breathing or wish to be sure you are using your diaphragm, this simple exercise will help. Lie on the floor with a book over your stomach. Inhale slowly, forcing the book to rise as the air enters. Next, exhale slowly, watching the book fall as the air is released. You may also do this exercise standing against a wall while holding a book at your midsection. After you have familiarized yourself with the area used and the flow of air, practice supporting words by first counting slowly and then moving on to simple sentences. Always keep your throat relaxed, supporting your speech with your diaphragm.

You will also find that the benefits of proper breathing do not begin on the platform: a few deep breaths before going to the podium will aid in fear control.

If you frequently speak in public or contemplate doing so at some future time, it will be worth your effort to master proper breath support. Any good basic speech textbook should have a section on the subject.

PROJECTION

In ordinary conversation we can speak very softly and still be heard. Not so when we are standing in front of an audience.

The burden for making your voice audible to everyone in the audience does *not* rest upon the person in the sound booth! *The speaker is solely responsible for making herself heard—period.* In a small classroom that usually is not a problem, unless the acoustics are horrible. But sooner or later you may face a situation such as the following:

- A roof-only campground "auditorium" on a cold, windy night
- A long, narrow room with a very high ceiling and no public address system
- A wrap-around auditorium with carpet on the floor and on the walls

Whatever the acoustical nightmare, *you must make your-self heard.* This is when diaphragmatic breathing becomes strategic. Without it, the effort to project can damage your vocal mechanism; with it, you will support your voice and allow it to reach as far as possible into the room. In many of these cases it is impossible for everyone to hear well, but by using proper breath support and articulating clearly, we can be assured that most will hear.

ARTICULATION

Though vocal sound is produced in the throat, it must be shaped into words. With tongue, lips, teeth, and palate we create recognizable speech; this is called *articulation.* After the early childhood thrill of learning to talk, after we survive that "fussy" English teacher, many of us relax into lazy enunciation or word formation. Taking those careless patterns to the platform can short-circuit communication.

Record one of your oral practice sessions. As you listen to the tape, concentrate on your articulation and enunciation. Are your words easy to understand? Do you slur sounds? Distort vowels? Drop final consonants? Most of us need to "crisp up" our diction for platform work. It will be impossible to help our hearers if they cannot understand what we are saying!

VOCAL GUIDELINES

The Christian woman's voice should *always* reflect femininity. One of my worst listening experiences came in a small room where a woman was conducting a workshop. She did not even finish her introduction before she shifted into a voice that would have put a circus barker to shame. She bellowed, boomed, and banged to an alarming extent. Each "whack!" on the podium made everyone in the room jump. Needless to say, we audience members went out with only our *nerves* affected!

Just as we avoid stentorian tones, we must also avoid syrupy speech. Sometimes Christian women speakers alter their voices drastically, apparently trying to sound pious or spiritual. This lends a false note to the speech, and the listener may stop listening because the speaker's voice does not ring true. It is important for each one of us simply to use our normal voice—the best it can be used.

USAGE

Good language usage in the United States is deteriorating. We have "anything goes" noun/verb agreement; we allow ourselves to pick up the abominable grammar of radio and television advertisements and we mimic the slang and jargon of actors. What a shame!

One benefit of modern living is the availability of education. How the Lord has blessed us in America! There are millions of women around the world who have absolutely no educational opportunity. But while education is a benefit, it also implies obligation: our learning should be utilized.

However careless you may have been in your school years about English, I would urge you to drag out those old textbooks and polish up your syntax, grammar, and pronunciation. Actually, whether or not you contemplate speaking in public, your language is having an effect on those around you.

Over and over God tells us in His word to *speak* for Him. Whether that be in private conversation or public address, our speech should exemplify good English. Every woman of the Lord should determine—in all of her speech—to use this wonderful English language *as accurately as she is able.* Why? For the American Christian, English is the *King's* English!

∾

"So likewise ye, except ye utter by the tongue words easy to be understood, how shall it be known what is spoken? For ye shall speak into the air."

I CORINTHIANS 14:9

10

THE MIND

THE&
MIND

It is important to remember, as you proceed along your speech pathway, that your audience is following wherever you go. You direct their attention by the focus of your own.

Having discussed in earlier chapters a number of things that should be considered or done during your preparation, I now want to make a recommendation for your actual speaking time: **Forget everything you thought about earlier.** Specifically,

- ꙮ Do **not** think about your stage fright.
- ꙮ Do **not** think of another speaker's technique.
- ꙮ Do **not** think about how you look.
- ꙮ Do **not** analyze your gestures.
- ꙮ Do **not** listen to your voice.
- ꙮ Do **not** worry about your grammar.

The point is, preparation time is the time to concentrate on the *technicalities* of speaking. Platform time is the time to concentrate on only one thing: **communicating your message.**

Bring all your mental focus to bear upon what you are saying. As you concentrate on your message, your audience will follow, step by step.

Once you have finished speaking, however, your mind will continue to have a message for you, whether you are simply sitting safely back onto your chair or while you socialize after the meeting. Your response to this internal message will often determine how you interact with your audience after you have finished speaking.

First, of course, there will be a natural relief that it is over. For the Christian, that relief should be accompanied by a silent expression of gratitude to the one who made it possible.

As you think back over your talk and realize the gaps or goofs that will have been there, do not whip yourself and feel like a failure, vowing never to try again. If you genuinely did your best, that is all you can do. Remember, God asks us to be faithful, not perfect. Learning to speak in public is much like learning to walk; you must try, try again. Each time you will do better, but you will never be free from an occasional stumble. Rather than mentally berating your stumblings, learn early to laugh at them. In fact, if you hit a major snag during the talk, do not be afraid to confess and laugh about it with the audience.

But more importantly, learn to commit those mistakes to the Lord. Even our misspoken words are under His control, and we must always recognize them as a reminder that "when I am weak, then He is strong." This perspective will help you avoid one of the most important pitfalls—pride. Keep your mental balance by combining common sense with practical spirituality. God tells us very clearly that He uses "the weak things of the world to confound the things which are mighty" (I Corinthians 1:27). God has deliberately chosen the weak and foolish things of the world as his vessels so "that no flesh should glory in his presence" (I Corinthians 1:29). How can we then become puffed up with our own self-importance, realizing that we are simply a vessel for the Master's use?

No matter how much some may gush about your presentations, take all human evaluations lightly. Take only God's evaluation seriously!

"That ye would walk worthy of God, who hath called you unto his kingdom and glory."

I THESSALONIANS 2:12

11

THE
FINAL WORD

THE FINAL WORD

I pray that the material presented in this little book has been clear and helpful. In moving to the close, I want to leave you a few gentle reminders.

The key ingredient in good manners is *sincerity*. Whatever your topic, wherever you are speaking, *be sincere*. Female audiences are not dumb; they see through the façade of an assumed, sweety-sweet facial expression or voice.

When you compliment your audience on the preparations, music, decorations, meal, and so forth that they have provided, be sincere; do not gush.

Mind your manners in that you *always* do the type of speech requested. Only an overblown ego would get up and say, "I was asked to speak about So-and-So, but I decided instead. . . ."

Good manners likewise honor the *occasion*. Whatever is special about this particular time, take note of it. That may mean having to construct an entirely new speech when you would rather make do with an old one.

Demonstrate your honor of *their* occasion by *your* compliance.

Abide by time limits. Period. Crashing through time barriers is for the crass. Too, some time limits may develop in the very midst of your speaking. The classic example could be a mother-daughter banquet when the toddler has fallen asleep on Susie's left shoulder, the aged mother on her right shoulder, and Susie herself is desperate for a restroom break. Obviously, you would be wise (and mannerly) to cut your talk short.

Finally, *be thankful*. Yes, genuinely, deeply *thankful* for *every* opportunity to talk to women. Be thankful to the Lord for allowing you this form of service; be thankful to the audience for inviting you and for listening.

Public speaking does, indeed, mean challenge. But it also means *opportunity and privilege*. So . . . when asked . . . in the Lord's power, with His help, for His glory, and to aid your listener along the bumpy, twisting path of Christian living, let your words be fitly spoken.

*"She openeth her mouth with wisdom: and
in her tongue is the law of kindness."*

PROVERBS 31:26